The Mighty Triceratops

Percy Leed

BUMBA BOOKS™

LERNER PUBLICATIONS ◆ MINNEAPOLIS

Note to Educators

Throughout this book, you'll find critical-thinking questions. These can be used to engage young readers in thinking critically about the topic and in using the text and photos to do so.

Lerner Publications Company
An imprint of Lerner Publishing Group, Inc.
241 First Avenue North
Minneapolis, MN 55401 USA

For reading levels and more information, look up this title at www.lernerbooks.com.

Main body text set in Helvetica Textbook Com Roman.
Typeface provided by Linotype AG.

Library of Congress Cataloging-in-Publication Data

Names: Leed, Percy, 1968– author.
Title: The mighty triceratops / Percy Leed.
Description: Minneapolis : Lerner Publications, [2022] | Series: Bumba books - mighty dinosaurs | Includes bibliographical references and index. | Audience: Ages 4–7 | Audience: Grades K–1 | Summary: "Triceratops had three horns on its head and hundreds of teeth in its mouth—yet in spite of its fierce appearance, it ate plants! Readers will love learning this and other fun facts about this dino"—Provided by publisher.
Identifiers: LCCN 2021010898 (print) | LCCN 2021010899 (ebook) | ISBN 9781728441030 (library binding) | ISBN 9781728444505 (ebook)
Subjects: LCSH: Triceratops—Juvenile literature.
Classification: LCC QE862.O65 L447 2022 (print) | LCC QE862.O65 (ebook) | DDC 567.915/8—dc23

LC record available at https://lccn.loc.gov/2021010898
LC ebook record available at https://lccn.loc.gov/2021010899

Manufactured in the United States of America
1-49873-49718-6/29/2021

Table of Contents

Horned Dino

Triceratops lived millions of years ago.

It is extinct.

This dinosaur was huge!

It weighed more than

11,000 pounds (4,990 kg).

Triceratops may have lived in groups. This may have helped it stay safe.

How might groups keep an animal safe?

Triceratops had three horns.

Two horns were above its eyes.

One was by its nose.

Sometimes Tyrannosaurus rex attacked! Triceratops fought with its horns.

How else do you think triceratops used its horns?

Triceratops had a frill.

This was a bone behind

its head. It may have

kept triceratops warm.

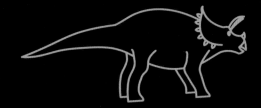

Triceratops walked on four legs.

Its legs were strong and sturdy.

Triceratops ate only plants.
It used its beak to pull plants
from the ground.

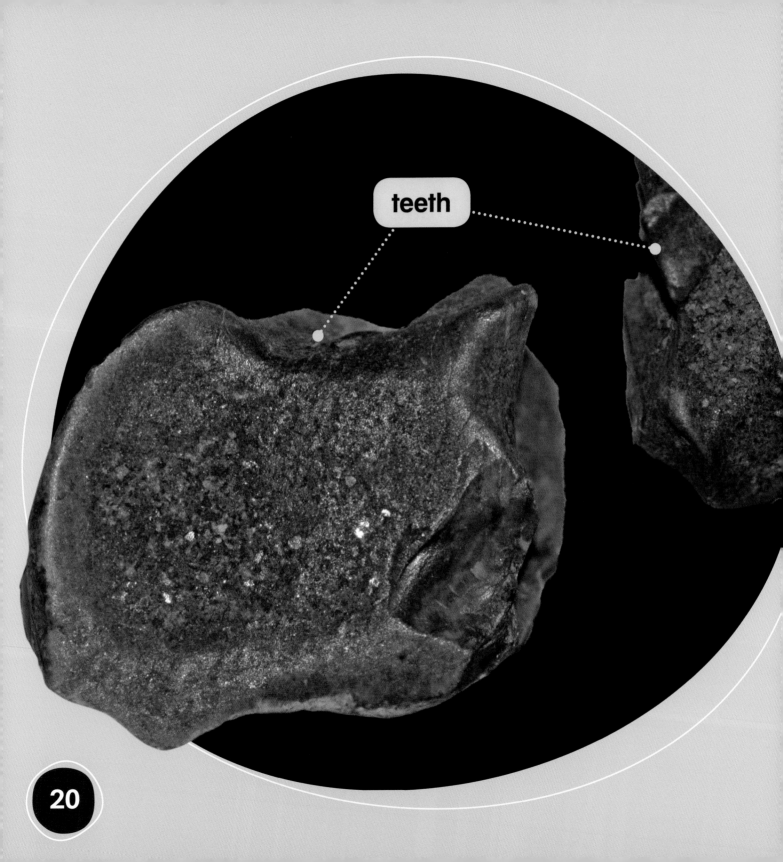

teeth

Triceratops had hundreds of teeth. The teeth had different parts. The parts helped triceratops chew plants.

Parts of a Triceratops

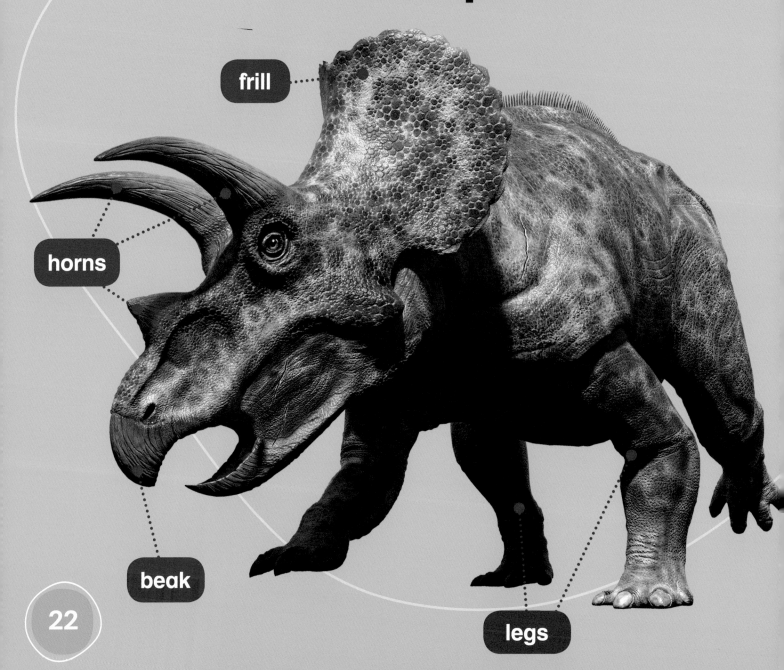

frill

horns

beak

legs

Picture Glossary

beak

the hard, pointed mouth of an animal

extinct

no longer alive

frill

a bone behind the head

horn

a hard, pointed growth on an animal

Learn More

Cole, Bradley. *Triceratops.* Minneapolis: Cody Koala, 2019.

Kaiser, Brianna. *The Mighty T. Rex.* Minneapolis: Lerner Publications, 2022.

Sabelko, Rebecca. *Triceratops.* Minneapolis: Bellwether Media, 2020.

Index

Photo Acknowledgments

Image credits: Elenarts/Shutterstock.com, pp. 5, 23; MARK GARLICK/SCIENCE PHOTO LIBRARY/Getty Images, p. 6; Daniel Eskridge/Shutterstock.com, p. 9; DM7/Shutterstock.com, pp. 10, 23; Martin Weber/Shutterstock.com, p. 13; Daniel Eskridge/Shutterstock.com, pp. 14, 23; Herschel Hoffmeyer/Shutterstock.com, p. 17; ExpressionImage/Shutterstock.com, pp. 18, 23; Ibe van Oort/Shutterstock.com, p. 20; ExpressionImage/Shutterstock.com, p. 22.

Cover image: Warpaint/Shutterstock.com.